Frogs

Aaron Frisch

CREATIVE EDUCATION

seedlings

Published by Creative Education
P.O. Box 227, Mankato, Minnesota 56002
Creative Education is an imprint of
The Creative Company
www.thecreativecompany.us

Design and production by Ellen Huber
Art direction by Rita Marshall
Printed in the United States of America

Photos by Bigstock (alptraum), Getty Images (Michael
Dunning, Gary Mezaros/Visuals Unlimited, Inc.),
iStockphoto (Sascha Burkard, Adam Gryko, Eric Isselée,
Oktay Ortakcioglu, Lee Pettet, spxChrome), National
Geographic Creative (HEIDI AND HANS-JURGEN KOCH/
MINDEN PICTURES), Photo Library (Oxford Scientific),
Shutterstock (Subbotina Anna, Sebastian Duda, Adam
Gryko, Jiri Hodecek, nodff, Dr. Morely Read), SuperStock
(Flirt, imagebroker.net), Veer (stevebyland)

Library of Congress Cataloging-in-Publication Data
Frisch, Aaron.
Frogs / Aaron Frisch.
p. cm. — (Seedlings)
Includes bibliographical references and index.
Summary: A kindergarten-level introduction to frogs,
covering their growth process, behaviors, the watery
places they call home, and such defining physical
features as their tongues.
ISBN 978-1-60818-458-3
1. Frogs—Juvenile literature. I. Title.

QL668.E2F755 2014
597.8'7—dc23   2013029067

CCSS: RI.K.1, 2, 3, 4, 5, 6, 7;
RI.1.1, 2, 3, 4, 5, 6, 7; RF.K.1, 3; RF.1.1

9 8 7 6 5 4 3

TABLE OF CONTENTS

Hello, frogs!

Frogs are animals that
are good at jumping.

Most frogs live by or in water.

Many frogs are green, yellow, or brown.

Some frogs
are many colors.

Frogs have
strong back legs.
Frogs that
swim a lot have
webbed feet.

Other frogs
have sticky feet.

Frogs eat bugs and worms.

Frogs use their long tongues to catch food.

13

Baby frogs are
called tadpoles.

Tadpoles look like fish.

Then they grow into adult frogs.

Frogs croak to find mates.

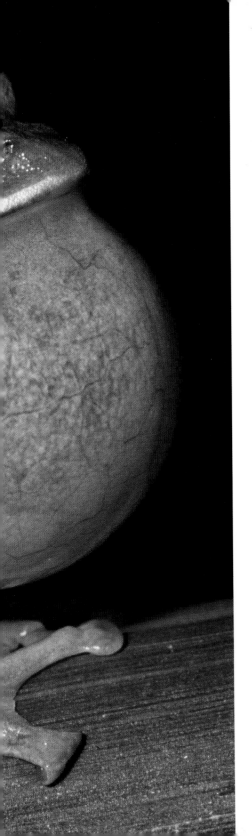

They jump
into water.
They look for
bugs to eat.

Goodbye, frogs!

Picture a Frog

sticky toe pad

webbed foot

leg

skin

nostril

eye

Words to Know

croak: make a loud, creaky sound

mates: other animals to have babies with

webbed: having toes connected by flat skin

Read More

Carney, Elizabeth. *Frogs!*
Washington, D.C.: National Geographic, 2009.

Green, Emily. *Frogs.*
Minneapolis: Bellwether Media, 2011.

Websites

DLTK's Crafts for Kids: Frog Activities
http://www.dltk-kids.com/animals/frogs.htm
Choose a frog craft to do. Or print and color frog pictures.

Frog Jigsaw Puzzle
http://www.first-school.ws/puzzlesonline/animals/frog.htm
Put together a puzzle with a picture of a frog.

Index